A CHRISTIAN'S RESPONSE TO DEATH

A 40-day Devotional for Turning your Loss into Gain

Maurice M. Harris, Sr.

This book is dedicated in loving memory of
Aaron Anthony Reid
Forever in our Hearts
May 23, 1994 ~ November 21, 2016

Foreword

The announcement of a new addition to the family is always exciting news for everyone. Then comes the trepidation that every expectant mother feels when wanting to do the right things as to not jeopardize the development of the little life growing within her body. What to eat? What not to eat? To exercise or not to exercise? Don't overdo it. What medications are safe? What vitamins or supplements to take? We know the baby is in there, but the fear of the unknown – the fact that we cannot see him or her – is a bit disconcerting at times. Even with all that, birth is a welcome event. Death, on the other hand, is not. But, just as with birth, death is a very real part of life. But when death comes, how do we handle it? My husband, who authored this book, has given Christians in this world the only right answer to that question within the pages of this book, *A Christian's Response to Death.*

Maurice Harris, Sr., is the best one to write this book because he is a born-again believer of 44 years and a pastor of 36 years. He is also a man after God's own heart, and a lover of God, His word, and His people. He is a graduate of Golden Gate Theological Seminary (currently Gateway Seminary) after having spent three years studying theology at Dallas Theological Seminary in Dallas, Texas. In other words, Maurice M. Harris, Sr., is a student of the Bible; however, his study did not end when he received his Master of Divinity degree. He is in the Bible just as much as the Bible is in him.

If you were drawn to this book, it is more likely than not that you or someone you know is currently experiencing the pain of the loss of a loved one. When my baby boy took his own life after just 22 short years on this earth, the pain of my loss was trying to consume me and drag me down into the great black hole of despair. But, my husband, Maurice M. Harris, Sr., grabbed my hand and insisted that I take a trip with him through the Scriptures, the Word of God, the Bible, to get me from where I was to where I needed to be. Reading this book will take you on a 40-day journey from a place of despair and unrest to a place of calm and peace. You will know that you have reached your destination when you realize that your loss has been turned into a gain through the power of the Word of God.

Alicia E. Harris

Thank you to the love of my life, Alicia,
my wonderful wife, whom I affectionately call, My Love,
who persevered through the challenges of
reading and editing this book that undoubtedly unlocked
devastating memories of a tragic loss all because
she knows that this work is much needed and will
bring a welcome relief to so many who are
suffering right now
after losing a loved one.

Table of Contents

INTRODUCTION

It was about 11:30 p.m., on Monday, November 22, 2016, when life, as my wife, Alicia, and I knew it, came to a sudden standstill with one dreaded phone call. I was in a deep sleep in my easy chair in our living room when I was suddenly jarred awake by unforgettable and unbelievable screams of despair and total horror. My wife, the very love of my life, whom I affectionately call "my love," had just received the horrific news that her beloved son, Aaron, had taken his own life at the tender age of 22 at about 9:00 p.m. that night while sitting in a car in the parking lot of his best friend's place of residence. It was the call that every parent dreads and it shook the very essence of her soul and spirit. My beautiful wife was devastated and experiencing emotions that she had never experienced in her entire life. She was in a place of deep, deep hurt, and emotional pain that I really can't explain or express with words. To put her condition into perspective, it was as if she was nonexistent within her own body as she fell completely limp and somewhat lifeless in my arms. I just held her tightly as we both grieved.

It was at that moment that deep within my spirit, I sensed God stirring up His word in a great way and, because my wife is very strong in her faith as a devout Christian, without hesitation, I began to console and comfort her with His word. Then, for the next 40 days, I walked her through the scriptures as it relates to how believers in the Bible responded to death when it came into their life. This book that you are holding in your hands was birthed out of that 40-day journey, and it is my privilege to share our very personal experience with those within the body of Christ who are hurting beyond measure due to grieving the loss of a loved one.

The death of a loved one is perhaps the most tragic, difficult, and emotionally strenuous experience that a person will face in his or her lifetime. However, for those of us who belong to God, we have consolation in knowing that He does not desire us to face this devastating experience alone and has thus declared in His word in 1 Peter 5:7, *"Cast all your anxiety upon Him, because He cares for you."*

It is His desire to walk you through this most difficult time in your life. He is the only one who can and will bring you through this painful journey of loss and completely restore you to a place of emotional stability. As my wife and I walked through this experience with the scriptures, I personally witnessed a spiritual metamorphosis take place in her, even though, just hours before she was physically and emotionally devastated and pretty much incapacitated. But as I poured the word into her over the ensuing 40 days, I saw how God began to restore her joy.

God has recorded in His word how He would bring us Christians through times of great loss. However, many of us have missed it because we either have not been taught or have been erroneously taught how to grieve as believers. What I discovered through the journey of walking my precious wife, my love, through the scriptures is that Christians are to focus on God during times of great pain and loss. This is how to turn the loss into a gain. The saints of old, whose experiences we will illuminate in the chapters to follow, accomplished this victory by praising God through the pain.

If you are reading this book and are in a place of grief and great pain right now, I invite you to nestle back into the arms of our loving Father as you embark on a 40-day journey back to the place of great joy as you allow the powerful word of God to turn the tragedy of your loss into a gain as it did for my love, Alicia.

JOB 1:19-22

19 And, behold, a great wind came from across the wilderness and struck the four corners of the house, and it fell on the young people, and they died, and I alone have escaped to tell you."
20 Then Job arose and tore his robe and shaved his head, and he fell to the ground and worshiped.
21 He said, "Naked I came from my mother's womb, and naked I shall return there. The Lord gave and the Lord has taken away. Blessed be the name of the Lord."
22 Through all this Job did not sin nor did he blame God.

DAY 1 The Christian's Response to Death

We, like Job, love God. We, like Job, fear God. We, like Job, pray for our children continually. (Job 1:1-5)

We, like Job, suffer loss and face tragedy. (Job 1:6-19)

We, like Job, are committed to God and respond from our faith and commitment to God by worshipping Him, praising His name, during the time of loss; and not sinning or blaming God. (Job 1:20-22)

During the time of great loss, Job teaches us as believers how we are to respond. He worshipped God and didn't blame God. He said, *"Naked I came from my mother's womb, and naked I shall return there. The Lord gave and the Lord has taken away. Blessed be the name of the Lord."* Through all this, Job did not sin, nor did he blame God. This is a right on time word from God after an authentic believer (Job) suffered great loss of precious loved ones.

Will you grieve? Absolutely! But you must grieve with your focus on your loving heavenly Father, not as if you have no hope!

To God be the Glory!

Reflections on God:

_____
_____
_____
_____
_____
_____
_____
_____
_____
_____
_____
_____
_____
_____
_____
_____
_____
_____
_____
_____
_____
_____
_____
_____
_____
_____
_____
_____
_____
_____
_____

Isaiah 6:1-8

In the year of King Uzziah's death I saw the Lord sitting on a throne, lofty and exalted, with the train of His robe filling the temple. 2Seraphim stood above Him, each having six wings: with two he covered his face, and with two he covered his feet, and with two he flew. 3And one called out to another and said, "Holy, Holy, Holy, is the Lord of hosts. The whole earth is full of His glory."

Day 2 The Christian's Focus when Faced with Death

The Lord seated on the throne! High and lifted up! He is holy, holy, holy! The Lord God is seated in a place of authority and majesty, and yet His presence (His train of His robe) fills the temple. His presence is in me as an authentic believer. I am a temple of the Holy Spirit – the presence of God!

Isaiah lost his cousin, King Uzziah. But, in his grief, he lifted his eyes, saw the Lord high and lifted up, and worshipped Him. He humbled himself before the Lord. (6:5) By worshipping the Lord in his time of grief, Isaiah became a powerful witness for the Lord! (6:8)

As an authentic believer, focusing on God in the face of tragedy, the loss of a dear loved one, turns the tragedy into triumph for the kingdom of God. Praise Him during this time of loss, and He will get the glory from your brokenness, and you will overcome your pain.

To God be Glorified!

Reflections on God:

_____
_____
_____
_____
_____
_____
_____
_____
_____
_____
_____
_____
_____
_____
_____
_____
_____
_____
_____
_____
_____
_____
_____
_____
_____
_____
_____
_____
_____
_____
_____
_____

2 Samuel 12:15-23

Then the Lord struck the child that Uriah's widow bore to David, so that he was very sick. 16David therefore inquired of God for the child; and David fasted and went and lay all night on the ground. 17The elders of his household stood beside him in order to raise him up from the ground, but he was unwilling and would not eat food with them. 18Then it happened on the seventh day that the child died. And the servants of David were afraid to tell him that the child was dead, for they said, "Behold, while the child was still alive, we spoke to him and he did not listen to our voice. How then can we tell him that the child is dead, since he might do himself harm!"
19But when David saw that his servants were whispering together, David perceived that the child was dead; so, David said to his servants, "Is the child dead?" And they said, "He is dead." 20So David arose from the ground, washed, anointed himself, and changed his clothes; and he came into the house of the Lord and worshiped. Then he came to his own house, and when he requested, they set food before him and he ate. 21Then his servants said to him, "What is this thing that you have done? While the child was alive, you fasted and wept; but when the child died, you arose and ate food?" 22He said, "While the child was still alive, I fasted and wept; for I said, 'Who knows, the Lord may be gracious to me, that the child may live.' 23But now he has died; why should I fast? Can I bring him back again? I will go to him, but he will not return to me."

Day 3 Death Compels the Child of God to Worship!

David, a servant chosen by God, was described as a man after God's own heart. When David's son died, like Job and Isaiah, he worshipped the Lord his God. As a believer, he had the right perspective. He did not grieve as if he had no hope. David knew that he would see his son again (vs. 23). When death hits the life of the authentic believer, the first thing the believer does is worship. (vs. 20). That worship continues through the entire grieving process. Prior to worship, David accepted the will of God to allow his son to die. (vs. 20) Then he worshipped, and then he went on living – he asked for food, and he ate (vs. 20).

David also had the proper perspective of the whole tragic event (vs. 23): *"I cannot bring him back. I shall go to him, but he will not return to me."*

Consecrate your heart on Him during this time of loss by magnifying Him through praise and worship, and His peace will help you to overcome your pain. He promises this in His word: *"I will keep in perfect peace those whose mind is stayed on me"* (Isaiah 26:3).

The joy of the Lord!

Reflections on God:

_____
_____
_____
_____
_____
_____
_____
_____
_____
_____
_____
_____
_____
_____
_____
_____
_____
_____
_____
_____
_____
_____
_____
_____
_____
_____
_____
_____
_____
_____

2 Kings 2:1-15

And it came about when the Lord was about to take up Elijah by a whirlwind to heaven, that Elijah went with Elisha from Gilgal. 2Elijah said to Elisha, "Stay here please, for the Lord has sent me as far as Bethel." But Elisha said, "As the Lord lives and as you yourself live, I will not leave you." So, they went down to Bethel. 3Then the sons of the prophets who were at Bethel came out to Elisha and said to him, "Do you know that the Lord will take away your master from over you today?" And he said, "Yes, I know; be still."

4Elijah said to him, "Elisha, please stay here, for the Lord has sent me to Jericho." But he said, "As the Lord lives, and as you yourself live, I will not leave you." So, they came to Jericho. 5The sons of the prophets who were at Jericho approached Elisha and said to him, "Do you know that the Lord will take away your master from over you today?" And he answered, "Yes, I know; be still." 6Then Elijah said to him, "Please stay here, for the Lord has sent me to the Jordan." And he said, "As the Lord lives, and as you yourself live, I will not leave you." So, the two of them went on.

7Now fifty men of the sons of the prophets went and stood opposite them at a distance, while the two of them stood by the Jordan. 8Elijah took his mantle and folded it together and struck the waters, and they were divided here and there, so that the two of them crossed over on dry ground.

9When they had crossed over, Elijah said to Elisha, "Ask what I shall do for you before I am taken from you." And Elisha said, "Please, let a double portion of your spirit be upon me." 10He said, "You have asked a hard thing. Nevertheless, if you see me when I am taken from you, it shall be so for you; but if not, it shall not be so." 11As they were going along and talking, behold, there appeared a chariot of fire and horses of fire which separated the two of them. And Elijah went up by a whirlwind to heaven. 12Elisha saw it and cried out, "My father, my father, the chariots of Israel and its horsemen!" And he saw Elijah no more. Then he took hold of his own clothes and tore them in two pieces.

13He also took up the mantle of Elijah that fell from him and returned and stood by the bank of the Jordan. 14He took the mantle of Elijah that fell from him and struck the waters and said, "Where is the Lord, the God of Elijah?" And when he also had struck the waters, they were divided here and there; and Elisha crossed over.

15Now when the sons of the prophets who were at Jericho opposite him saw him, they said, "The spirit of Elijah rests on Elisha." And they came to meet him and bowed themselves to the ground before him.

DAY 4 Elisha's Response to the Passing of Elijah

Elijah walked with God. Elisha walked with Elijah and God. Although Elisha knew God was going to take Elijah, when it happened, his initial response was shock (vs.12a); followed by grief (vs.12a). Then Elisha continued to follow God.

As long as we live on this earth, we know death is imminent. When and to whom it will strike, we don't know; but when it occurs, our initial response is shock. Then, after the shock, we mourn. However, what we do next is indicative of whether we have the right perspective or not during this time of loss. The right perspective for the believer is to look to the Lord God for further instruction and direction. (vs.14)

Elisha worshipped and went on living as he looked to the Lord God. (vs.12b) As believers, when we are faced with death, it is imperative that we turn our focus on our God and worship Him who is the God of all comfort and strength. The Apostle Paul gives some tremendous insight to this critical point in 1 Thessalonians 5:18 when he points our focus on the right place: *"In everything give thanks; for this is God's will for you in Christ Jesus."* You are not thankful *because* of the loss of your precious loved one; however, you are thankful that the all-powerful God, the one who can take away all your pain, is living inside of you.

Turn to Him by worshipping Him during this time of great pain and loss. He will bring you to a place of comfort and joy. This is His will for you.

Reflections on God:

_____
_____
_____
_____
_____
_____
_____
_____
_____
_____
_____
_____
_____
_____
_____
_____
_____
_____
_____
_____
_____
_____
_____
_____
_____
_____
_____
_____
_____
_____
_____
_____
_____

John 11:14-35

14 So Jesus then said to them plainly, "Lazarus is dead, 15 and I am glad for your sakes that I was not there, so that you may believe; but let us go to him." 16 Therefore Thomas, who is called Didymus, said to his fellow disciples, "Let us also go, so that we may die with Him." 17 So when Jesus came, He found that he had already been in the tomb four days. 18 Now Bethany was near Jerusalem, about two miles off; 19 and many of the Jews had come to Martha and Mary, to console them concerning their brother. 20 Martha therefore, when she heard that Jesus was coming, went to meet Him, but Mary stayed at the house. 21 Martha then said to Jesus, "Lord, if You had been here, my brother would not have died. 22 Even now I know that whatever You ask of God, God will give You."

*23 Jesus said to her, "Your brother will rise again." 24Martha said to Him, "I know that he will rise again in the resurrection on the last day." 25Jesus said to her, "I am the resurrection and the life; he who believes in Me will live even if he dies, 26and everyone who lives and believes in Me will never die. Do you believe this?" 27She said to Him, "Yes, Lord; I have believed that You are the Christ, the Son of God, even He who comes into the world."28 When she had said this, she went away and called Mary her sister, saying secretly, "The Teacher is here and is calling for you." 29 And when she heard it, she *got up quickly and was coming to Him.30 Now Jesus had not yet come into the village but was still in the place where Martha met Him. 31 Then the Jews who were with her in the house, and consoling her, when they saw that Mary got up quickly and went out, they followed her, supposing that she was going to the tomb to weep there. 32 Therefore, when Mary came where Jesus was, she saw Him, and fell at His feet, saying to Him, "Lord, if You had been here, my brother would not have died." 33 When Jesus therefore saw her weeping, and the Jews who came with her also weeping, He was deeply moved in spirit and was troubled, 34 and said, "Where have you laid him?" They said to Him, "Lord, come and see." 35 Jesus wept.*

DAY 5 A Healthy Response to Death (Mary & Martha)

Grieving is a real process that everyone who experiences loss goes through. However, the child of God turns to God and gains an understanding of how to worship Him through the grieving process. On the past few days of our journey, we have seen several witnesses who worshiped God through their grief: Job, Isaiah, David, and Elisha. Today, we look at Mary and Martha.

Mary and Martha both had the right perspective regarding death. They grieved, but they worshipped and focused on the Lord Jesus Christ. Even Jesus wept (11:35), but not as one who had no hope. (In fact, He was getting ready to raise Lazarus from the dead). As believers, our hope is in the one who says, *"He is the resurrection and the life"* (vs. 25). Our hope is that our loved ones whom we lost believed in Him as we do, and then we can say like David, *"We can't bring them back to us, but we can go where they are."*

As believers, we praise Him when death comes because we are of the firm belief that He is our perfect healer and comforter. He is the resurrection. He conquered death, hell, and the grave. Through our praise, He will lift us out of the pain and grief. Placing us in a place of peace and rest as only He can as our powerful healer.

Reflections on God:

_____
_____
_____
_____
_____
_____
_____
_____
_____
_____
_____
_____
_____
_____
_____
_____
_____
_____
_____
_____
_____
_____
_____
_____
_____
_____
_____
_____
_____
_____
_____
_____
_____
_____
_____
_____

Matthew 9:18-26

18 While He was saying these things to them, a synagogue official came and bowed down before Him, and said, "My daughter has just died; but come and lay Your hand on her, and she will live." 19 Jesus got up and began to follow him, and so did His disciples.

20 And a woman who had been suffering from a hemorrhage for twelve years, came up behind Him and touched the fringe of His cloak; 21 for she was saying to herself, "If I only touch His garment, I will get well." 22 But Jesus turning and seeing her said, "Daughter, take courage; your faith has made you well." At once the woman was made well.

23 When Jesus came into the official's house and saw the flute-players and the crowd in noisy disorder, 24 He said, "Leave; for the girl has not died, but is asleep." And they began laughing at Him. 25 But when the crowd had been sent out, He entered and took her by the hand, and the girl got up. 26 This news spread throughout all that land.

DAY 6 The Behavior of the Believer when Faced with Death

It is never God's intention for us to react to situations as the world and paganistic culture does no matter if the situation is good or bad. *"Let this mind be in you that is also in Christ."* (Philippians 2:5)

In Matthew 9, the ruler's daughter died, and his first reaction was to seek out the Lord (vs. 18), and he worshipped Him (vs. 18). He recognized that the Lord was in control of life and death (vs. 18). This is the reaction of the authentic believer – one who knows the Lord. A non-believer reacts differently e.g., ranting, raving, blaming, not wanting to live, etc.

This ruler, a man by the name of Jairus, joins the others who had the right perspective when faced with death: Job, Isaiah, David, Elisha, Mary, and Martha. The Lord Jesus wants the believer to be removed from naysayers – those who are causing commotion and noisy disorder. It is His desire that the believer focuses on the power and sovereignty of God (vs. 23-26).

The spiritual insight in Matthew 9:18-26 is worship. Jairus knew who to worship during his time of great loss. The behavior of the authentic believer when faced with death is to worship the Most- High God, our Lord and Savior Jesus Christ. He is our great God of comfort and sweet peace during the most painful and difficult time in life. He will bring you out of your grief. Trust Him!

Reflections on God:

_____
_____
_____
_____
_____
_____
_____
_____
_____
_____
_____
_____
_____
_____
_____
_____
_____
_____
_____
_____
_____
_____
_____
_____
_____
_____
_____
_____
_____
_____
_____
_____
_____

Luke 23:44-56

44 It was now about the sixth hour, and darkness fell over the whole land until the ninth hour, 45 because the sun was obscured; and the veil of the temple was torn in two. 46 And Jesus, crying out with a loud voice, said, "Father, into Your hands I commit My spirit." Having said this, He breathed His last. 47 Now when the centurion saw what had happened, he began praising God, saying, "Certainly this man was innocent." 48 And all the crowds who came together for this spectacle, when they observed what had happened, began to return, beating their breasts.

49 And all His acquaintances and the women who accompanied Him from Galilee were standing at a distance, seeing these things. 50 And a man named Joseph, who was a member of the Council, a good and righteous man 51 (he had not consented to their plan and action), a man from Arimathea, a city of the Jews, who was waiting for the kingdom of God; 52 this man went to Pilate and asked for the body of Jesus.

53 And he took it down and wrapped it in a linen cloth and laid Him in a tomb cut into the rock, where no one had ever lain. 54 It was the preparation day, and the Sabbath was about to begin.

55 Now the women who had come with Him out of Galilee followed and saw the tomb and how His body was laid. 56 Then they returned and prepared spices and perfumes.

DAY 7 When Faced with Death, the Believer is Drawn to Worship

At the death of Jesus, we see praise (vs. 47); and we see a righteous man who kept his eye on the prize: *"The Kingdom of God"* (vs. 51). Also, we see His followers continuing in their service to Him (vs. 53-56).

W	Continue praising God - The Centurion
O	Continue looking to God - Joseph
	Continue serving God - Jesus' Followers
R	1Thessalonians 5:16-19 – instructions to
S	the believer:
H	"Rejoice Always" (vs.16)
	"Pray without Ceasing" (vs. 17)
I	"Give Thanks in Everything" (vs. 18)
P	"Quench not the Spirit" (vs. 19)

Reflections on God:

_____
_____
_____
_____
_____
_____
_____
_____
_____
_____
_____
_____
_____
_____
_____
_____
_____
_____
_____
_____
_____
_____
_____
_____
_____
_____
_____
_____
_____
_____
_____
_____
_____

2 Samuel 12:18-23

18 Then it happened on the seventh day that the child died. And the servants of David were afraid to tell him that the child was dead, for they said, "Behold, while the child was still alive, we spoke to him and he did not listen to our voice. How then can we tell him that the child is dead, since he might do himself harm!" 19 But when David saw that his servants were whispering together, David perceived that the child was dead; so, David said to his servants, "Is the child dead?" And they said, "He is dead." 20 So David arose from the ground, washed, anointed himself, and changed his clothes; and he came into the house of the Lord and worshiped. Then he came to his own house, and when he requested, they set food before him and he ate. 21 Then his servants said to him, "What is this thing that you have done? While the child was alive, you fasted and wept; but when the child died, you arose and ate food." 22 He said, "While the child was still alive, I fasted and wept; for I said, 'Who knows, the Lord may be gracious to me, that the child may live.' 23 But now he has died; why should I fast? Can I bring him back again? I will go to him, but he will not return to me."

DAY 8 A Revisit of David's Story: The Death of His Son

When his son died, DAVID WORSHIPPED!
He arose from the ground.
He washed his face and anointed himself.
He went to the house of God and worshipped.
He asked for food and ate.

David had the right perspective when he was faced with death. He said, *"Can fasting and weeping bring my son back? He is not coming back to me but, I will go to where he is."* (vs. 23)

Consecrate your heart on Him during this time of loss by magnifying Him through praise and worship and you will overcome your pain with His peace. *"I will keep those in perfect peace whose mind is stayed on me."* (Isaiah 26:3)

Reflections on God:

_____
_____
_____
_____
_____
_____
_____
_____
_____
_____
_____
_____
_____
_____
_____
_____
_____
_____
_____
_____
_____
_____
_____
_____
_____
_____
_____
_____
_____
_____
_____

Matthew 8:5-13

5 And when Jesus entered Capernaum, a centurion came to Him, imploring Him, 6 and saying, "Lord, my servant is lying paralyzed at home, fearfully tormented." 7 Jesus said to him, "I will come and heal him." 8 But the centurion said, "Lord, I am not worthy for You to come under my roof, but just say the word, and my servant will be healed. 9 For I also am a man under authority, with soldiers under me; and I say to this one, 'Go!' and he goes, and to another, 'Come!' and he comes, and to my slave, 'Do this!' and he does it." 10 Now when Jesus heard this, He marveled and said to those who were following, "Truly I say to you, I have not found such great faith with anyone in Israel. 11 I say to you that many will come from east and west, and recline at the table with Abraham, Isaac and Jacob in the kingdom of heaven; 12 but the sons of the kingdom will be cast out into the outer darkness; in that place there will be weeping and gnashing of teeth." 13 And Jesus said to the centurion, "Go; it shall be done for you as you have believed." And the servant was healed that very moment.

DAY 9 When Death Comes, Take God at His Word

When death comes into your life, take God at his word and act on your faith. So far, we looked at the following believers and their response to death:

Job (Job 1)
David (2 Samuel 12:15-23)
Isaiah (Isaiah 6:1-8)
Elisha (2 Kings 2:1-15)
Mary & Martha (John 11:14-35)
Jairus (Matthew 9:18-26)
The Centurion, Joseph, and the followers of Jesus
(Luke 23:44-56)

In today's passage, Matthew 8:5-13, the centurion had the faith to take the Lord at His word, and he walked in it. His faith was so remarkable that Jesus marveled: *"Now when Jesus heard this, He marveled and said to those who were following, I have not found such great faith with anyone in Israel."* (vs. 10)

In the middle of despair, this believing centurion acted on his faith in the Lord. He acted on what he said. When death comes into your life, remember what the Lord promised you and act on your faith in Him. Take Him at His word. The Lord promises to take us through all our trials, tribulations, heartaches, heartbreaks, disappointments, breakups, and breakdowns. *"Many are the afflictions of the righteous, But the LORD delivers him out of them all."* (Psalm 34:19)

Worship Him dear people of God. Jesus honored the faith of the centurion (vs.13). He will honor your faith during this difficult time of great loss. Trust Him, act on your faith, and WORSHIP! Follow the examples of your fellow brothers and sisters who are recorded in the Word of God.

Reflections on God:

_____
_____
_____
_____
_____
_____
_____
_____
_____
_____
_____
_____
_____
_____
_____
_____
_____
_____
_____
_____
_____
_____
_____
_____
_____
_____
_____
_____
_____
_____
_____
_____
_____
_____
_____

Ruth 1:1-22

*Now it came about in the days when the judges governed,
that there was a famine in the land. And a certain man of
Bethlehem in Judah went to sojourn in the land of Moab with his
wife and his two sons. 2 The name of the man was Elimelech,
and the name of his wife, Naomi; and the names of his two sons
were Mahlon and Chilion, Ephrathites of Bethlehem in Judah.
Now they entered the land of Moab and remained there. 3 Then
Elimelech, Naomi's husband, died; and she was left with her two
sons. 4 They took for themselves Moabite women as wives; the
name of the one was Orpah and the name of the other Ruth.
And they lived there about ten years. 5 Then both Mahlon and
Chilion also died, and the woman was bereft of her two children
and her husband. 6 Then she arose with her daughters-in-law
that she might return from the land of Moab, for she had heard
in the land of Moab that the Lord had visited His people in giving
them food. 7 So she departed from the place where she was,
and her two daughters-in-law with her; and they went on the
way to return to the land of Judah. 8 And Naomi said to her two
daughters-in-law, "Go, return each of you to her mother's
house. May the Lord deal kindly with you as you have dealt with
the dead and with me. 9 May the Lord grant that you may find
rest, each in the house of her husband." Then she kissed them,
and they lifted up their voices and wept. 10 And they said to her,
"No, but we will surely return with you to your people." 11 But
Naomi said, "Return, my daughters. Why should you go with
me? Have I yet sons in my womb, that they may be your
husbands? 12 Return, my daughters! Go, for I am too old to
have a husband. If I said I have hope, if I should even have a
husband tonight and also bear sons, 13 would you therefore
wait until they were grown? Would you therefore refrain from
marrying? No, my daughters; for it is harder for me than for you,
for the hand of the Lord has gone forth against me." 14 And
they lifted up their voices and wept again; and Orpah kissed her
mother-in-law, but Ruth clung to her.
15 Then she said, "Behold, your sister-in-law has gone back
to her people and her gods; return after your sister-in-law." 16
But Ruth said, "Do not urge me to leave you or turn back from
following you; for where you go, I will go, and where you lodge, I*

will lodge. Your people shall be my people, and your God, my God. 17 Where you die, I will die, and there I will be buried. Thus, may the Lord do to me, and worse, if anything but death parts you and me." 18 When she saw that she was determined to go with her, she said no more to her. 19 So they both went until they came to Bethlehem. And when they had come to Bethlehem, all the city was stirred because of them, and the women said, "Is this Naomi?" 20 She said to them, "Do not call me Naomi; call me Mara, for the Almighty has dealt very bitterly with me. 21 I went out full, but the Lord has brought me back empty. Why do you call me Naomi, since the Lord has witnessed against me and the Almighty has afflicted me?"

22 So Naomi returned, and with her Ruth the Moabitess, her daughter-in-law, who returned from the land of Moab. And they came to Bethlehem at the beginning of barley harvest.

DAY 10 How the Believer Responds to Death: A Look at Naomi

When we look at the book of Ruth as it describes the death of Naomi's husband and two sons, we see that Naomi kept her focus on God and moved forward with her life in God. Immediately after the death of her two sons, the scripture records her mindset and heart at the time of her devastating loss of her two sons: *"Then she arose with her daughters-in-law that she might return from the land of Moab, for she had heard in the land of Moab that the LORD had visited His people in giving them food."* (vs. 6)

Naomi continued to move forward with her daughter-in-law, Ruth. If we fast forward to the end of the story, we see how God was working in the midst of this tragedy as we see that Ruth married Boaz who fathered Obed, who fathered Jesse, who fathered David. Our Lord and Savior Jesus Christ came from the lineage of David

Yes, Naomi experienced a great deal of pain and loss, but she did not allow that to anesthetize her from moving forward in her life with God! In the midst of her tremendous loss, she worshipped God in her very unique way. She kept the right perspective as the other believers that we have previously examined in this devotional study of worship during the time of precious loss. In thus so doing, we see how God was at work in a mighty way through her tragedy and loss. Worship Him, for this is His will for you!

Reflections on God:

_____

_____

_____

_____

_____

_____

_____

_____

_____

_____

_____

_____

_____

_____

_____

_____

_____

_____

_____

_____

_____

_____

_____

_____

_____

_____

_____

_____

_____

_____

_____

_____

_____

Luke 9:59-60

59 And He said to another, "Follow Me." But he said, "Lord, permit me first to go and bury my father." 60 But He said to him, "Allow the dead to bury their own dead; but as for you, go and proclaim everywhere the kingdom of God."

DAY 11 How the Believer Responds to Death: Continuing to Proclaim the Kingdom of God

One of the followers of Jesus (an authentic believer) wanted to stop and bury his father, but in essence the LORD Jesus Christ, said nothing is more important than proclaiming the gospel. We continue to proclaim the gospel in the midst of our grief.

The LORD's perspective and purpose for us as believers in the midst of loss is for us to worship Him and keep our focus on Him and the Kingdom. As believers, during the time of loss, God wants to use our testimony of worship to draw others to Him and His Kingdom. When we worship Him in the midst of our grief, the focus is moved from our grief to His glory and Kingdom. Worship Him and let Him use you as the sweet instrument that you are to Him.

Reflections on God:

_____
_____
_____
_____
_____
_____
_____
_____
_____
_____
_____
_____
_____
_____
_____
_____
_____
_____
_____
_____
_____
_____
_____
_____
_____
_____
_____
_____
_____
_____
_____
_____

Psalm 23

The Lord is my shepherd, I shall not want.2 He makes me lie down in green pastures; He leads me beside quiet waters.3 He restores my soul; He guides me in the paths of righteousness for His name's sake.
4 Even though I walk through the valley of the shadow of death, I fear no evil, for You are with me; Your rod and Your staff, they comfort me.5 You prepare a table before me in the presence of my enemies; You have anointed my head with oil; My cup overflows.6 Surely goodness and loving-kindness will follow me all the days of my life.

DAY 12 The Believer's Response and Recovery: Moving On

The 23rd Psalm serves as a psalm of worship when a believer understand its meaning. The 23rd Psalm demonstrates, displays, and describes for us believers that we are completely covered by God for our frailties, foes, and future. Psalm 23 will cause believers to worship God in the time of our weakness when we have the right perspective of the purpose of this great Psalm. The LORD is your shepherd who desires to lead you during this time of hurt. Just worship Him as your providing and guiding shepherd.

Death does not anesthetize the believer. Death does not stop the believer from worshipping God. Death does not stop the believer from living for the Lord. Death does not stop the testimony of the believer concerning the power of God. Trials, tribulations, and tragedies strengthen the testimony of the believer.

In recap, we have situation after situation showing how God led the believer through the process of mourning the death of a loved one through the wonderful gift of worship! He is our shepherd: The shepherd of Psalm 23. He leads us through difficult circumstances of life. One of our greatest weapons is WORSHIP!

Reflections on God:

_____
_____
_____
_____
_____
_____
_____
_____
_____
_____
_____
_____
_____
_____
_____
_____
_____
_____
_____
_____
_____
_____
_____
_____
_____
_____
_____
_____
_____
_____
_____
_____
_____
_____
_____
_____

Acts 7:54-60; 8:2-4

54 When the members of the Sanhedrin heard this, they were furious and gnashed their teeth at him. 55 But Stephen, full of the Holy Spirit, looked up to heaven and saw the glory of God, and Jesus standing at the right hand of God. 56 "Look," he said, "I see heaven open and the Son of Man standing at the right hand of God."

57 At this they covered their ears and, yelling at the top of their voices, they all rushed at him, 58 dragged him out of the city and began to stone him. Meanwhile, the witnesses laid their coats at the feet of a young man named Saul.

59 While they were stoning him, Stephen prayed, "Lord Jesus, receive my spirit." 60 Then he fell on his knees and cried out, "Lord, do not hold this sin against them." When he had said this, he fell asleep.

On that day a great persecution broke out against the church in Jerusalem, and all except the apostles were scattered throughout Judea and Samaria. 2 Godly men buried Stephen and mourned deeply for him. 3 But Saul began to destroy the church. Going from house to house, he dragged off both men and women and put them in prison.

DAY 13 The Believer's Natural Response to Death – 1

This passage talks about the stoning of Stephen, who was a man of God, and the very natural response of other believers. (8:2) In the process of moving on with life, it is a very natural response to lament over the death of a precious loved one. However, as believers we must move forward with our life by focusing on the God of our Salvation. And as you have witnessed in the life of the believers recorded in scripture, this is accomplished through the beautiful and powerful act of worship. The believers in this text worshipped after experiencing the death of Stephen. The Bible records their worship in this way: "*They went about preaching the word.* (8:4)

We as believers are to hold on to and proclaim the word of God. Our weapon is the word of God. The word of God instructs us to worship Him always. "*Rejoice in the Lord always; again, I will say, rejoice!*" (Philippians 4:4)

Reflections on God:

_____
_____
_____
_____
_____
_____
_____
_____
_____
_____
_____
_____
_____
_____
_____
_____
_____
_____
_____
_____
_____
_____
_____
_____
_____
_____
_____
_____
_____
_____
_____

2 Kings 4:1-7

The wife of a man from the company of the prophets cried out to Elisha, "Your servant my husband is dead, and you know that he revered the Lord. But now his creditor is coming to take my two boys as his slaves."2 Elisha replied to her, "How can I help you? Tell me, what do you have in your house? Your servant has nothing there at all," she said, "except a small jar of olive oil.3 Elisha said, "Go around and ask all your neighbors for empty jars. Don't ask for just a few. 4 Then go inside and shut the door behind you and your sons. Pour oil into all the jars, and as each is filled, put it to one side." 5 She left him and shut the door behind her and her sons. They brought the jars to her and she kept pouring. 6 When all the jars were full, she said to her son, "Bring me another one. But, he replied, "There is not a jar left." Then the oil stopped flowing.7 She went and told the man of God, and he said, "Go, sell the oil and pay your debts. You and your sons can live on what is left."

DAY 14 The Believer's Natural Response to Death – 2

Everybody's initial reaction to the news of death is different. Some people cry out; some people stare off into space; some people are very silent, and some people are very vocal. However, every believer's initial response after the initial reaction is to turn to God and worship. The believer's worship is a testimony of his faith in God, belief in God, and trust in God. Having this right perspective, the believer is able to move forward rejoicing, praying, and being thankful. (1 Thessalonians 5:16-18).

In today's passage, a woman's husband died. Her husband was a God-fearing servant of God (vs. 1). This passage is an example of a woman of God who is now a widow who moved forward with her life. Faced with difficulty with financial matters, instead of losing hope with the loss of her husband, she sought out the man of God, Elisha, for direction. (Her trust was in God. Trust in God is a great form of worship.) Death does not anesthetize the believer from continuing to worship God. The believer worships Him by trusting Him and seeking Him for direction in his or her life and moving forward to live for His glory!

The widow doesn't go to just any man to help her, she goes to the man of God. She exhibits trust in God by seeking out the man of God. She exhibits faith in God by obeying the man of God. She exhibits a desire to want to continue to live by worshipping God. She took God at his word and followed through with the actions which is a picture of a believer moving forward. (vs. 5-7) This is working faith. This is a beautiful and sweet exhibition of worship.

Reflections on God:

_____
_____
_____
_____
_____
_____
_____
_____
_____
_____
_____
_____
_____
_____
_____
_____
_____
_____
_____
_____
_____
_____
_____
_____
_____
_____
_____
_____
_____
_____
_____
_____
_____
_____
_____

2 Kings 4:8-30

8 One day Elisha went to Shunem. And a well-to-do woman was there, who urged him to stay for a meal. So, whenever he came by, he stopped there to eat. 9 She said to her husband, "I know that this man who often comes our way is a holy man of God. 10 Let's make a small room on the roof and put in it a bed and a table, a chair, and a lamp for him. Then he can stay there whenever he comes to us." 11 One day when Elisha came, he went up to his room and lay down there. 12 He said to his servant Gehazi, "Call the Shunammite." So, he called her, and she stood before him. 13 Elisha said to him, "Tell her, 'You have gone to all this trouble for us. Now what can be done for you? Can we speak on your behalf to the king or the commander of the army?'" She replied, "I have a home among my own people." 14 "What can be done for her?" Elisha asked. Gehazi said, "She has no son, and her husband is old." 15 Then Elisha said, "Call her." So, he called her, and she stood in the doorway. 16 "About this time next year," Elisha said, "you will hold a son in your arms." "No, my lord!" she objected. "Please, man of God, don't mislead your servant!" 17 But the woman became pregnant, and the next year about that same time she gave birth to a son, just as Elisha had told her. 18 The child grew, and one day he went out to his father, who was with the reapers. 19 He said to his father, "My head! My head!" His father told a servant, "Carry him to his mother. 20 After the servant had lifted him up and carried him to his mother, the boy sat on her lap until noon, and then he died. 21 She went up and laid him on the bed of the man of God, then shut the door and went out.22 She called her husband and said, "Please send me one of the servants and a donkey so I can go to the man of God quickly and return."23 "Why go to him today?" he asked. "It's not the New Moon or the Sabbath."

"That's all right," she said. 24 She saddled the donkey and said to her servant, "Lead on; don't slow down for me unless I tell you." 25 So she set out and came to the man of God at Mount Carmel. When he saw her in the distance, the man of God said to his servant Gehazi, "Look! There's the Shunammite. 26 Run to meet her and ask her, 'Are you all right? Is your husband all right? Is your child all right?'"

"Everything is all right," she said. 27 When she reached the man of God at the mountain, she took hold of his feet. Gehazi came over to push her away, but the man of God said, "Leave her alone! She is in bitter distress, but the Lord has hidden it from me and has not told me why."

28 "Did I ask you for a son, my lord?" she said. "Didn't I tell you, 'Don't raise my hopes'? 29 Elisha said to Gehazi, "Tuck your cloak into your belt, take my staff in your hand and run. Don't greet anyone you meet, and if anyone greets you, do not answer. Lay my staff on the boy's face."

30 But the child's mother said, "As surely as the Lord lives and as you live, I will not leave you." So, he got up and followed her.

DAY 15 The Believer's Response to Death: The Shunammite Woman

Elisha was a man of God. The Shunammite woman recognized him as the man of God. (vs. 9) She had no children, but Elisha prophesied that she would have a son. (vs. 16) When her son was a young lad, he died. (vs. 20) Her response was to seek out the man of God. (vs. 22) She had the right perspective to seek God through the man of God. Elisha prophesied that she would have a son. (Life was given to the woman by God.) The right perspective is to recognize that God has power over life, that is to give life and to take it away. When a believer experiences death in his or her life the natural response is to seek out God and worship Him!

We do witness in this passage the natural reaction of the woman as she was in bitter distress. (vs. 27) However, she never gave up on God, stating that she would not leave the man of God. (vs. 30) This is a picture of her putting her complete trust in God through the man of God. I will worship until you bless me! Dear woman or man of God worship Him until He bless you. Worship Him until your pain, your grief turns into joy and complete comfort.

Reflections on God:

_____
_____
_____
_____
_____
_____
_____
_____
_____
_____
_____
_____
_____
_____
_____
_____
_____
_____
_____
_____
_____
_____
_____
_____
_____
_____
_____
_____
_____
_____
_____
_____
_____
_____
_____
_____

Psalm 34

I will bless the Lord at all times; His praise shall continually be in my mouth.2 My soul will make its boast in the Lord; The humble will hear it and rejoice.3 O magnify the Lord with me, And let us exalt His name together.

4 I sought the Lord, and He answered me, And delivered me from all my fears.5 They looked to Him and were radiant, And their faces will never be ashamed.6 This poor man cried, and the Lord heard him And saved him out of all his troubles.7 The angel of the Lord encamps around those who fear Him, And rescues them. O taste and see that the Lord is good; How blessed is the man who takes refuge in Him!9 O fear the Lord, you His saints; For to those who fear Him there is no want.10 The young lions do lack and suffer hunger; But they who seek the Lord shall not be in want of any good thing.11 Come, you children, listen to me; I will teach you the fear of the Lord.12 Who is the man who desires life and loves length of days that he may see good?13 Keep your tongue from evil and your lips from speaking deceit.14 Depart from evil and do good; Seek peace and pursue it.

15 The eyes of the Lord are toward the righteous and His ears are open to their cry. The face of the Lord is against evildoers, to cut off the memory of them from the earth.17 The righteous cry, and the Lord hears and delivers them out of all their troubles.18 The Lord is near to the brokenhearted and saves those who are crushed in spirit.

19 Many are the afflictions of the righteous, but the Lord delivers him out of them all.20 He keeps all his bones, not one of them is broken.21 Evil shall slay the wicked, and those who hate the righteous will be condemned.22 The Lord redeems the soul of His servants, and none of those who take refuge in Him will be condemned.

DAY 16 Moving Forward after the Death of a Precious Loved One - 1

Psalm 34 is David's song of worship unto God. Over the past two weeks, we saw in the word where the believers had the right perspective after the death of their loved ones: even through bereavement they worshipped God. Worship is a key given to us by God in order for us to move forward through any circumstance, including death.

Worship points us to God, which is, of course, what He desires. He does not want us to turn to others or to other modalities in place of Him! Yes, He places people in our life to help us through; however, He is first, and foremost and He takes precedence, so we go to Him first and we stay with Him always. How do we stay with Him always?

1 Thessalonians 5:16-19 -
Rejoice!
Pray!
Give thanks!
Quench not the Spirit!

Psalm 34 is a song of worship unto God from David. Will weeping come? Yes, weeping will come. However, worship needs to follow weeping. Worship according to Psalm 34:

"Bless the Lord at all times" (vs. 1)
"Magnify the Lord, Exalt His name" (vs. 3)
"Seek the Lord" (vs. 4)
"Take refuse in the Lord" (vs. 8)
"Fear (reverence) the Lord" (vs. 9)
"Seek peace" (vs. 14)
"Cry out to the Lord" (vs. 17)

The believer's worship results in:

"Radiance" (vs. 5)
"Encampment by the Lord" (vs. 7)
"Deliverance" (vss. 7, 17, 19)
"No lack" (vs. 9)
"The eyes of the Lord toward the believer, and His ears toward the believer's cry" (vs. 15)
"Nearness of the Lord to the broken-hearted and salvation of the crushed in spirit" (vs. 18)
"Redemption, and not condemnation" (vs. 22)

God is faithful as we move forward from weeping to worship. Psalm 34 is a song that David sung to the Lord God after coming through a difficult situation. David recognized that God brought him through, so, he sang unto the Lord.

Take the example of David, dear people of God, and worship!

Worship

Reflections on God:

_____

_____

_____

_____

_____

_____

_____

_____

_____

_____

_____

_____

_____

_____

_____

_____

_____

_____

_____

_____

_____

_____

_____

_____

_____

_____

_____

_____

_____

_____

_____

_____

_____

_____

Psalm 103

Bless the Lord, O my soul, and all that is within me, bless His holy name. 2 Bless the Lord, O my soul, and forget none of His benefits; 3 Who pardons all your iniquities, who heals all your diseases; 4 Who redeems your life from the pit, who crowns you with loving-kindness and compassion; 5 Who satisfies your years with good things, so that your youth is renewed like the eagle.

6 The Lord performs righteous deeds and judgments for all who are oppressed. 7 He made known His ways to Moses, His acts to the sons of Israel. 8 The Lord is compassionate and gracious, slow to anger and abounding in lovingkindness. 9 He will not always strive with us, nor will He keep His anger forever. 10 He has not dealt with us according to our sins, nor rewarded us according to our iniquities. 11 For as high as the heavens are above the earth, so great is His loving-kindness toward those who fear Him. 12 As far as the east is from the west, so far has He removed our transgressions from us. 13 Just as a father has compassion on his children, So the Lord has compassion on those who fear Him. 14 For He Himself knows our frame; he is mindful that we are but dust.

15 As for man, his days are like grass; as a flower of the field, so he flourishes. 16 When the wind has passed over it, it is no more, and its place acknowledges it no longer. 17 but the loving-kindness of the Lord is from everlasting to everlasting on those who fear Him, and His righteousness to children's children, 18 to those who keep His covenant and remember His precepts to do them.

19 The Lord has established His throne in the heavens, and His sovereignty rules overall. 20 Bless the Lord, you His angels, mighty in strength, who perform His word, obeying the voice of His word! 21 Bless the Lord, all you His hosts, you who serve Him, doing His will. 22 bless the Lord, all you works of His, in all places of His dominion; bless the Lord, O my soul!

DAY 17 Moving Forward after the Death of a Precious Loved One - 2

With this Psalm of David, we continue to see David's worship unto the Lord God even after all he endured. Like David, in the face of adversity, tragedy, testing, and disappointments, the believer continues to:

"Bless the Lord with all" (v. 1)
"Remember all that the Lord does" (vss. 2-5; 22)
"Remember His grace and mercy" (v. 8)
"Remember His great love" (v. 11)
"Remember that the Lord is Sovereign" (v. 19)

We move forward by blessing the Lord and worshipping with all that is in us. Why? Because the believer has that right perspective of who God is. God is:

The forgiver of all our iniquity (v. 3)
The healer of our diseases (v. 3)
The Redeemer of life (v. 4)
The giver of good (v. 5)
The worker of righteousness and justice (v. 6)
Merciful and gracious (v. 8)
Sovereign (v. 19)

The believer does not lose perspective as to who God is in difficult times. This is how the believer is able to move forward and continue to worship.

Reflections on God:

_____
_____
_____
_____
_____
_____
_____
_____
_____
_____
_____
_____
_____
_____
_____
_____
_____
_____
_____
_____
_____
_____
_____
_____
_____
_____
_____
_____
_____
_____
_____
_____
_____

Philippians 3:12-16

12 Not that I have already obtained it or have already become perfect, but I press on so that I may lay hold of that for which also I was laid hold of by Christ Jesus. 13 Brethren, I do not regard myself as having laid hold of it yet; but one thing I do: forgetting what lies behind and reaching forward to what lies ahead, 14 I press on toward the goal for the prize of the upward call of God in Christ Jesus. 15 Let us therefore, as many as are perfect, have this attitude; and if in anything you have a different attitude, God will reveal that also to you; 16 however, let us keep living by that same standard to which we have attained.

DAY 18 Pressing on through Grief

Because He Lives, I can face tomorrow.
Because He Lives, all fear is gone.
Because He Lives, I know He holds the future;
and life is worth the living just because He Lives!

Christ laid hold of me. I love Him because He first loved me (1 John 4:19). He keeps hold of me. 1 Peter 1:5 says, *"We are kept by His mighty power through faith unto salvation."* Christ laid hold of me to be like Him. The goal of my living is to be like Christ. The prize is being like Christ.

Verse 1 of chapter 3 of Philippians says, *"Rejoice in the Lord."* This alone puts the believer's mind into the right perspective in order to be able to "press on" (vs. 12); to "keep pulling forward" (vs. 13); and to "hold true," or "keep living" (vs. 16).

So, rejoice and press on by worshipping our God who lives in you for the purpose of transforming your tragedy to triumph and joy once again!

Reflections on God:

_____
_____
_____
_____
_____
_____
_____
_____
_____
_____
_____
_____
_____
_____
_____
_____
_____
_____
_____
_____
_____
_____
_____
_____
_____
_____
_____
_____
_____
_____
_____
_____
_____

1 John 1:1-4

What was from the beginning, what we have heard, what we have seen with our eyes, what we have looked at and touched with our hands, concerning the Word of Life— 2 and the life was manifested, and we have seen and testify and proclaim to you the eternal life, which was with the Father and was manifested to us— 3 what we have seen and heard we proclaim to you also, so that you too may have fellowship with us; and indeed our fellowship is with the Father, and with His Son Jesus Christ. 4 These things we write, so that our joy may be made complete.

DAY 19 Witnessing through Grief

Witnesses testify to the truth. Believers are witnesses for the Lord. Believers give testimony of who God is and how He is working in our life. Other believers pick up on the deep, genuine gladness that goes beyond natural happiness and those who do not yet know the Lord will find themselves hungering for the relationship that the believer has. In that way, they will be drawn to His Spirit.

Witnessing is an overflow of the personal relationship with Jesus Christ that is conforming the believer into the image of Christ even through tragic events, trials, and tribulations. As we allow the Holy Spirit to increasingly express His life and power through us, contagious joy will be "fruit" of His indwelling presence. (vs. 4)

The Apostle John's purpose for writing this text to believers was so, *"that our joy may be made complete."* My purpose for writing this devotional is so that your joy will continue to be manifested during this time of great loss through the power of your glorious witness as you worship His ever presence in your life of tremendous hurt.

Let others see Him through your worship!

Reflections on God:

_____
_____
_____
_____
_____
_____
_____
_____
_____
_____
_____
_____
_____
_____
_____
_____
_____
_____
_____
_____
_____
_____
_____
_____
_____
_____
_____
_____
_____
_____
_____
_____
_____

Galatians 4:6-7

6 Because you are sons, God has sent forth the Spirit of His Son into our hearts, crying, "Abba! Father!" 7 Therefore you are no longer a slave, but a son; and if a son, then an heir through God.

Ephesians 1:1-14

Paul, an apostle of Christ Jesus by the will of God, To the saints who are at Ephesus and who are faithful in Christ Jesus: 2 Grace to you and peace from God our Father and the Lord Jesus Christ. 3 Blessed be the God and Father of our Lord Jesus Christ, who has blessed us with every spiritual blessing in the heavenly places in Christ, 4 just as He chose us in Him before the foundation of the world, that we would be holy and blameless before Him. In love
5 He predestined us to adoption as sons through Jesus Christ to Himself, according to the kind intention of His will, 6 to the praise of the glory of His grace, which He freely bestowed on us in the Beloved. 7 In Him we have redemption through His blood, the forgiveness of our trespasses, according to the riches of His grace 8 which He lavished on us. In all wisdom and insight 9 He made known to us the mystery of His will, according to His kind intention which He purposed in Him
10 with a view to an administration suitable to the fullness of the times, that is, the summing up of all things in Christ, things in the heavens and things on the earth. In Him 11 also we have obtained an inheritance, having been predestined according to His purpose who works all things after the counsel of His will, 12 to the end that we who were the first to hope in Christ would be to the praise of His glory. 13 In Him, you also, after listening to the message of truth, the gospel of your salvation—having also believed, you were sealed in Him with the Holy Spirit of promise, 14 who is given as a pledge of our inheritance, with a view to the redemption of God's own possession, to the praise of His glory.

Day 20 Continuing to Live for Christ when Death Comes

As believers, we are no longer slaves but sons of God and heirs through God. (Gal. 4:7) *"However, at the time, when you did not know God, you were slaves to those which by nature are no gods."* (Gal. 4:8) Before the Lord saved us, we were subject to act as the world, to whom we were enslaved. We had no control over the flesh; however, now that we are believers in the risen Christ, we are no longer slaves to this flesh. We have been set free. We now operate in the spirit.

When death comes, God has given us the ability through the power of worship to glorify Him in the most tragic and difficult times in our life as believers. Whereas non-believers respond to the death of a loved one with behavior that is completely out of control – exhibiting evidence of hopelessness. As believers our response to the death of a loved one is completely the opposite. *"Blessed be the God and Father of our Lord Jesus Christ, who has blessed us with every spiritual blessing in the heavenly places in Christ."* (Eph.1:3)

This verse simply means that the believer worships God who has blessed us with every spiritual blessing in the heavenly places in Christ. Paul further states in verse 12, *"To the end that we who were the first to hope in Christ would be to the praise of His glory."* Yes, when death comes, we hurt and we weep, but not without hope. Our hope is in Christ. Therefore, we do not focus on the loss, but we focus on Christ through worshipping. Remember, we are not enslaved to the flesh. We have been set free.

During the period of grief, do what God has equipped you to do by setting you free. Worship Him!

Reflections on God:

_____
_____
_____
_____
_____
_____
_____
_____
_____
_____
_____
_____
_____
_____
_____
_____
_____
_____
_____
_____
_____
_____
_____
_____
_____
_____
_____
_____
_____
_____
_____
_____
_____

Philippians 4:4-7

4 Rejoice in the Lord always; again, I will say, rejoice! 5 Let your gentle spirit be known to all men. The Lord is near. 6 Be anxious for nothing, but in everything by prayer and supplication with thanksgiving let your requests be made known to God. 7 And the peace of God, which surpasses all comprehension, will guard your hearts and your minds in Christ Jesus.

DAY 21 Continuing on: Worship is the Key

Worship for the believer is not limited to time or place. Worship for the believer is a state of being – it is a consistent attitude – shared and aided by the Holy Spirit of God. How does the believer press on through all situations?

> Rejoice in the Lord. When? ALWAYS! (vs. 4)
> Rejoice: delight in leaning on the Lord.
> Delight: to find joy in Him. When? ALWAYS!
> In whom? The LORD!
> In the job? No! In The LORD!
> In money? No! In The LORD!
> In friends? No! In The LORD!
> In the loss of a loved one? No! The LORD!

These things can easily take precedence in the mind and, as believers, we are reminded to worship and *"again to rejoice."* (vs. 4) Being in this state will usher in the peace of God to guard the heart and mind of the believer from his or her flesh (fleshly comprehension). (vs. 7) The believer rejoices in the peace of God and focuses on the things of God. What things? Things that are pure, true, honorable, just, lovely, excellent, praiseworthy, commendable (or of good report). All these things add up to Christ Jesus. So, essentially, we are commanded to think on Him.

The believer who is in a state of worship will rejoice and will think on these things (Christ Jesus) by the power of the Holy Spirit. (vs. 8) To think on other things is to not be in the state of worship. The private and consistent attitude of the believer's worship is powerful during the time of great loss.

Worship the Christ and His peace will take over your grief and pain.

Reflections on God:

_____
_____
_____
_____
_____
_____
_____
_____
_____
_____
_____
_____
_____
_____
_____
_____
_____
_____
_____
_____
_____
_____
_____
_____
_____
_____
_____
_____
_____
_____
_____
_____

1 Thessalonians 5:16-19

16 Rejoice always; 17 pray without ceasing; 18 in everything give thanks; for this is God's will for you in Christ Jesus. 19 Do not quench the Spirit.

DAY 22 The Christian and Difficult Times

How does the Christian – the follower of Christ, who is also the imitator of Christ – make it through difficult times? Difficult times will come, and the loss of a precious loved one will come. This is a reality for everyone, both Christians and non-Christians alike. It is the responsibility for us as believers to allow God to use the difficult times to mold and shape us unto the very image of Jesus Christ.

God wants the world to always see Jesus in us and especially during difficult times. How do we allow that to happen? The last imperative in the 4 verses of 1 Thessalonians is really the first imperative (vs. 19): *"Quench not the Spirit."*

Allow the Holy Spirit of God to rise and reign in you during difficult times by doing what He desires for you to do and that is worship! *"For this is God's will for you."* (vs. 18)

Child of God, with His power, we are able to obey the other commands, *"Rejoice in the Lord."* (vs. 16); *"Pray without ceasing."* (vs. 17) *"Be thankful and give thanks in all things."* (vs. 18) Your focus is on Him and Him alone.

Worship Him in difficult times and He will lift you up, for this is His will for you!

Reflections on God:

_____
_____
_____
_____
_____
_____
_____
_____
_____
_____
_____
_____
_____
_____
_____
_____
_____
_____
_____
_____
_____
_____
_____
_____
_____
_____
_____
_____
_____
_____
_____
_____

2 Corinthians 10:5-6

5 We are destroying speculations and every lofty thing raised up against the knowledge of God, and we are taking every thought captive to the obedience of Christ, 6 and we are ready to punish all disobedience, whenever your obedience is complete.

Day 23 The Christian and Obedience

Obedience for the believer is more than just following rules. People in general break rules and laws. Believers and non-believers break all kinds of rules and laws probably every day. One rule that comes to mind is no sampling of bulk food items at the grocery store. One law that comes to mind is the speed law. The speed limits are broken as if they don't exist.

However, obedience for the believer is deeper than following a rule or law. Obedience for the believer is to actively and attentively listen and submit to the authority and will of God. This is unequivocally true for the believer during the loss of a precious loved one. It is God's will for you to worship during this most difficult and trying time in your life. However, flesh will revolt against the knowledge of God, seeking to cause you to be disobedient to our God during this most critical time. Obedience in this text, in the Greek is *hupakouo* (hoop-ak-oo-o): meaning to act under the authority or under the hearing of.

Disobedience starts in the mind. Our actions are controlled by our minds. 2 Corinthians 10:5-6, tells us to *"take every thought captive to obey Christ, being ready to punish every disobedience when your obedience is complete."* This is an active, ongoing lifestyle of the believer. The word says "every thought" whether it be our own thought or the erroneous thought of others. The believer is under the submission of God the Father, Jesus Christ, the Son, and the Holy Spirit. The Godhead! During the time of great loss flesh will rise up against the knowledge of God, and seek to pull you from your only strengthen which is worship. Be ready to punish this disobedience with obedience by worshipping the God who is the only one that's able to lift you out of this awful time of hurt and despair.

To God be the Glory!

Reflections on God:

_____

_____
_____
_____
_____
_____
_____
_____
_____
_____
_____
_____
_____
_____
_____
_____
_____
_____
_____
_____
_____
_____
_____
_____
_____
_____
_____
_____
_____
_____
_____
_____
_____
_____
_____

1 Thessalonians 1:2-7

2 We give thanks to God always for all of you, making mention of you in our prayers; 3 constantly bearing in mind your work of faith and labor of love and steadfastness of hope in our Lord Jesus Christ in the presence of our God and Father, 4 knowing, brethren beloved by God, His choice of you; 5 for our gospel did not come to you in word only, but also in power and in the Holy Spirit and with full conviction; just as you know what kind of men we proved to be among you for your sake. 6 You also became imitators of us and of the Lord, having received the word in much tribulation with the joy of the Holy Spirit, 7 so that you became an example to all the believers in Macedonia and in Achaia.

DAY 24 A Baby Church's Example of a Mature Believer

As a believer matures in his/her relationship and walk with the Lord, the following description Paul said of the Church in Thessalonica will also apply: They exemplified:

Work of faith
Labor of love
Steadfastness of hope
Imitators of the Lord

Paul summed it up in verse 7: *"You became an example to all believers..."* The church to whom he was speaking was an example even in the face of extreme persecution. This is a young (baby) church. A believer who is new in Christ can be an example to all believes by the power of the Holy Spirit at work within the believer as the believer yields to and quenches not the Spirit, which leads to worship, in the form of rejoicing always, praying without ceasing, being thankful in everything, even in the midst of great pain and loss. This behavior is what the Apostle Paul describes as leading to works of faith, labors of love, steadfastness of hope and, ultimately, imitators of the Lord. Wow! This is good news, people of God.

Worship! Worship! Worship!

Reflections on God:

_____
_____
_____
_____
_____
_____
_____
_____
_____
_____
_____
_____
_____
_____
_____
_____
_____
_____
_____
_____
_____
_____
_____
_____
_____
_____
_____
_____
_____
_____
_____
_____
_____
_____

Matthew 5:1-16

1 When Jesus saw the crowds, He went up on the mountain; and after He sat down, His disciples came to Him. 2 He opened His mouth and began to teach them, saying,
3 "Blessed are the poor in spirit, for theirs is the kingdom of heaven.
4 "Blessed are those who mourn, for they shall be comforted.
5 "Blessed are the gentle, for they shall inherit the earth.
6 "Blessed are those who hunger and thirst for righteousness, for they shall be satisfied.
7 "Blessed are the merciful, for they shall receive mercy.
8 "Blessed are the pure in heart, for they shall see God.
9 "Blessed are the peacemakers, for they shall be called sons of God. 10 "Blessed are those who have been persecuted for the sake of righteousness, for theirs is the kingdom of heaven. 11 "Blessed are you when people insult you and persecute you, and falsely say all kinds of evil against you because of Me. 12 Rejoice and be glad, for your reward in heaven is great; for in the same way they persecuted the prophets who were before you. 13 "You are the salt of the earth; but if the salt has become tasteless, how can it be made salty again? It is no longer good for anything, except to be thrown out and trampled underfoot by men. 14 "You are the light of the world. A city set on a hill cannot be hidden; 15 nor does anyone light a lamp and put it under a basket, but on the lampstand, and it gives light to all who are in the house. 16 Let your light shine before men in such a way that they may see your good works and glorify your Father who is in heaven.

DAY 25 Witnessing through Testing and Pain

God saves us to be a witness for Him. In giving us Jesus Christ, His Son, He gave us His All. A believer has the Holy Spirit of God through the gift of salvation to help him or her witness through times of testing. Witness what? Be a witness for the one who saved us and gave us the power to endure testing with JOY! Worshipping is the key.

Jesus opens His Sermon on the Mount by revealing the character of the believer: Blessed! Blessed means happy, joyful. This is a state of being (beatitude) of the believer. Jesus lists the types of testing the believer will face brokenness, mourning, times when we are to be merciful, temptation, wars, persecution, revilers, and evil utterances (slander). However, Jesus says through all of this, *"Rejoice and be glad."* (vs. 12) Jesus says we are salt (meaning that our life is to remain pure); we are light (meaning that our life is to illuminate the power, which is the light that dwells within us). (vss. 13-14)

A powerful witness of our Lord is magnified when we worship Him through our testing and pain. The light of His glory shines through us and the blessing of our God comes through with great victory in us and for all who encounter us. Jesus highlights this great truth when He commands us in verse 16 to essentially worship: *"Let your light shine before men in such a way that they may see your good works and glorify your Father who is in heaven."*

Worship, dear people of God. Be a witness through times of testing and pain!

Reflections on God:

_____
_____
_____
_____
_____
_____
_____
_____
_____
_____
_____
_____
_____
_____
_____
_____
_____
_____
_____
_____
_____
_____
_____
_____
_____
_____
_____
_____
_____
_____
_____
_____
_____
_____

1 Peter 2:1-12

1 Therefore, putting aside all malice and all deceit and hypocrisy and envy and all slander, 2 like newborn babies, long for the pure milk of the word, so that by it you may grow in respect to salvation, 3 if you have tasted the kindness of the Lord. 4 And coming to Him as to a living stone which has been rejected by men but is choice and precious in the sight of God, 5 you also, as living stones, are being built up as a spiritual house for a holy priesthood, to offer up spiritual sacrifices acceptable to God through Jesus Christ. 6 For this is contained in Scripture: "Behold, I lay in Zion a choice stone, a precious corner stone, And he who believes in Him will not be disappointed." 7 This precious value, then, is for you who believe; but for those who disbelieve, "The stone which the builders rejected, This became the very corner stone,"8 and, "A stone of stumbling and a rock of offense"; for they stumble because they are disobedient to the word, and to this doom they were also appointed. 9 But you are a chosen race, a royal priesthood, a holy nation, a people for God's own possession, so that you may proclaim the excellencies of Him who has called you out of darkness into His marvelous light; 10 for you once were not a people, but now you are the people of God; you had not received mercy, but now you have received mercy. 11 Beloved, I urge you as aliens and strangers to abstain from fleshly lusts which wage war against the soul. 12 Keep your behavior excellent among the Gentiles, so that in the thing in which they slander you as evildoers, they may because of your good deeds, as they observe them, glorify God in the day of visitation."

DAY 26 The Believer's Life is for God's Glory

When we become a believer, we lose our identity and pick up God's. Born-again believers are saints of God with God's DNA. When people look at the believer, they don't see "an old sinner," but they see Him. They will see our good works and glorify Him. Peter says the believer, like Christ, is like a living stone. A living stone being built up as a spiritual house to be a *"holy priesthood."* (vs. 5)

This description is far from being "just a sinner." Peter also goes on to describe the believer in verse 9 *"as a chosen race, a royal priesthood, a holy nation."* We believers live in this so that we fulfill our purpose for being here: *"To proclaim the excellences of Him who called us out of darkness into His marvelous light."* The converted life of the believer is evident through worship. We always worship Him for His provision and transformation of our life.

Believers are controlled by the Holy Spirit to live for God and to worship Him at all times for His goodness, especially in times of loss and hurt. Sinners (unbelievers) are controlled by the flesh to live for this world and respond to loss and pain as the world does – without hope. Believers abstain from the passions of the flesh (vs. 11) and live for the passion of the Father. God has set you free from following your flesh in the time of great loss and hurt. (vs. 12) Glorify God! Worship, instead of following your flesh into despair, misery, and hopelessness!

To God be the Glory!

Reflections on God:

_____
_____
_____
_____
_____
_____
_____
_____
_____
_____
_____
_____
_____
_____
_____
_____
_____
_____
_____
_____
_____
_____
_____
_____
_____
_____
_____
_____
_____
_____
_____
_____

John 14:1

"Do not let your hearts be troubled. You believe in God; believe also in me."

DAY 27 Faith in Christ Leads to Comfort and Worship in the Time of Loss

This single verse is a great motivation for an authentic believer. It draws him or her into a place of comfort and worship during the time of great loss of a precious loved one. These are the powerful and comforting words of our Lord and Savior Jesus Christ who, in a few days from the time of that writing, will be leaving these precious disciples whom He loved very dearly after spending every moment with them for three years in a very powerful spiritual and intimate relationship.

In the disciples' minds and hearts, He is leaving them forever and they are devastated! So, from the passionate heart of Jesus, He tells them to remind them of their faith: *"Do not let your hearts be troubled. You believe in God; believe also in me."* So, the disciples' focus changed from devastation and grief to comfort and worship through faith.

The imperative point is to *"not let your hearts be troubled."* Why? Because your God and Lord will always be there with you and for you particularly in the times of difficulty and loss. You must put your faith to work by worshipping our Lord and God.

As we ponder the life of the saints of God previously mentioned in this devotional who chose to worship His glorious existence in their life as opposed to focusing on the loss and hurt, think on this thought: our Lord has come that our joy may be made complete. 1 John 1:3-4 declares: *"What we have seen and heard we proclaim to you also, so that you too may have fellowship with us; and indeed, our fellowship is with the Father, and with His Son Jesus Christ. These things we write, so that our joy may be made complete."*

As an authentic believer we have complete joy in Him, no matter what we face. We must put our faith to work, and joy will manifest itself in us and through us. That is through the powerful vehicle of worship.

Reflections on God:

_____
_____
_____
_____
_____
_____
_____
_____
_____
_____
_____
_____
_____
_____
_____
_____
_____
_____
_____
_____
_____
_____
_____
_____
_____
_____
_____
_____
_____
_____
_____
_____
_____
_____
_____
_____

James 5:13

"Is anyone among you suffering? Then he must pray. Is anyone cheerful? He is to sing praises."

DAY 28 In the Midst of Suffering, a Believer is Called to Worship

The context of this beautiful passage captures believers who were under a severe amount of persecution. So severe that the persecution brought many of them to a place of spiritual weakness and placed a tremendous amount of emotional stress on their souls. For many of the believers during this devastating period in their life, it simply became unbearable and extremely difficult for them to move forward in life. So, James the Pastor of the Jerusalem Church, wrote to these scattered believers and called them to worship in this very insightful and enlighten verse: *"Is anyone among you suffering? Then he must pray. Is anyone cheerful? He is to sing praises."*

The Greek structure of this verse when translated means if a believer is experiencing emotional distress, he or she is to worship! That is to offer prayers continually to God and to sing psalms of God unto God. Worship lifts and restores the soul of the believer.

When a believer loses a precious loved one, he or she experiences pain and distress to no end. In some cases, it becomes somewhat unbearable and presents a tremendous challenge for the believer to move forward in life. So, listen to the voice of James as he encouraged the believers of old in James 5:13, which now reminds you to worship our God in Spirit and in truth.

Dearly beloved, as you are experiencing the pain of the loss of you loved one, turn to what our God has given you to bring you out of this pain and distress. You will turn your pain to gain if you worship Him through prayer and psalm.

To God be the glory!

Reflections on God:

_____
_____
_____
_____
_____
_____
_____
_____
_____
_____
_____
_____
_____
_____
_____
_____
_____
_____
_____
_____
_____
_____
_____
_____
_____
_____
_____
_____
_____
_____
_____
_____
_____
_____
_____
_____

2 Corinthians 1:3-5

"Blessed be the God and Father of our Lord Jesus Christ, the Father of mercies and God of all comfort, who comforts us in all our affliction so that we will be able to comfort those who are in any affliction with the comfort with which we ourselves are comforted by God. For just as the sufferings of Christ are ours in abundance, so also our comfort is abundant through Christ."

Day 29 God of all Comfort

When the loss of a loved one becomes a reality, we are immediately bombarded with deep emotional stress and pain. During this tragic time in the life of the believer, the Apostle Paul in 2 Corinthians 1:3-5 reminds the child of God where he or she can find help and comfort and that is through the power of personal worship with the God of all comfort.

During his Christian journey, the Apostle Paul had to turn to the God of all comfort for worship on many occasions because of the deep pain brought on him due to great personal loss and abandonment. One of those such occasions is recorded in 2 Timothy 4:16-18:

> *"At my first defense no one supported me, but all deserted me; may it not be counted against them. But the Lord stood with me and strengthened me, so that through me the proclamation might be fully accomplished, and that all the Gentiles might hear; and I was rescued out of the lion's mouth. The Lord will rescue me from every evil deed and will bring me safely to His heavenly kingdom; to Him be the glory forever and ever, Amen."*

That is why he could declare in verse 3, *"Blessed be the God and Father of our Lord Jesus Christ, the Father of mercies and God of all comfort."* This word blessed in the Greek is εὐλογητός, meaning to praise, pertaining to being worthy of praise or commendation—'one to be praised.' When translated, the Apostle Paul simply worshipped the Lord Jesus Christ and the Father during his time of great loss, pain, and abandonment.

My brother or my sister, during this time of your great loss and pain, take the example of the Apostle Paul and bless the God and Father of our Lord Jesus Christ, the Father of mercies and God of all comfort. This will enable you to turn your pain into gain in the power and might of our Great God and our Lord Jesus Christ!

Reflection on God:

_____
_____
_____
_____
_____
_____
_____
_____
_____
_____
_____
_____
_____
_____
_____
_____
_____
_____
_____
_____
_____
_____
_____
_____
_____
_____
_____
_____
_____
_____
_____
_____
_____
_____

Romans 8:35-39

35 Who will separate us from the love of Christ? Will tribulation, or distress, or persecution, or famine, or nakedness, or peril, or sword? 36 Just as it is written,
"For Your sake we are being put to death all day long;
We were considered as sheep to be slaughtered."
37 But in all these things we overwhelmingly conquer through Him who loved us. 38 For I am convinced that neither death, nor life, nor angels, nor principalities, nor things present, nor things to come, nor powers, 39 nor height, nor depth, nor any other created thing, will be able to separate us from the love of God, which is in Christ Jesus our Lord.

Day 30 You are More than a Conqueror in Christ Jesus

In this text, the Bible declares that every authentic believer is a conqueror, and not only a conqueror, but a super conqueror no matter what you are facing in life. The words in verse 37 mean to *overwhelmingly* conquer, meaning to overpower in victory, to be abundantly victorious, and to prevail mightily in all that you encounter in life. In these five incredible verses, the Apostle Paul gives his powerful and personal testimony from one who had personally experienced super victory in life's struggles. He experienced great loss through the persecution of countless individuals who were precious in his life. How did he survive the loss and become a super conqueror when death came into his life? He worshipped! Listen to his words of worship in verses 38-39 and let them minister to your soul:

"For I am convinced that neither death,
nor life, nor angels, nor principalities,
nor things present, nor things to come,
nor powers, nor height, nor depth, nor
any other created thing, will be able
separate us from the love of God, which
is in Christ Jesus our Lord."

In your loss and great pain today, God has made you victor. Worship Him and turn you pain into gain. Worship Him with these rhetorical words of the text: "*Who will separate us from the love of Christ? Will tribulation, or distress, or persecution, or famine, or nakedness, or peril, or sword?*" The answer is "**NOTHING!**" Man of God, woman of God, worship and let Him lift you from a place of sadness to a place of victory in Him. You are a SUPER CONQUEROR! To God be the Glory!

Reflection on God:

_____
_____
_____
_____
_____
_____
_____
_____
_____
_____
_____
_____
_____
_____
_____
_____
_____
_____
_____
_____
_____
_____
_____
_____
_____
_____
_____
_____
_____

Psalm 121:1-8

1 I will lift up my eyes to the mountains; From where shall my help come? 2 My help comes from the Lord, who made heaven and earth. 3 He will not allow your foot to slip; He who keeps you will not slumber. 4 Behold, He who keeps Israel will neither slumber nor sleep. 5 The Lord is your keeper; the Lord is your shade on your right hand. 6 The sun will not smite you by day, nor the moon by night. 7 The Lord will protect you from all evil; He will keep your soul. 8 The Lord will guard your going out and your coming in from this time forth and forever.

Day 31 Look to the Lord for your Help

Other than Psalm 23, Psalm 121 is perhaps the most referred to Psalm and read during homegoing services of precious loved ones. This gracious Psalm is called an "exquisite Psalm" and a "sweet outpouring of quiet trust." It is a Psalm of comfort and triumph when a believer is faced with a tremendous challenge in life that brings on immense pain and hurt that requires help that only God can meet.

Like Psalm 23, this is a Psalm describing the personal and intimate relationship between God and the believer with the use of personal pronouns in verses 1 & 2: *"I will lift up my eyes to the mountains; From where shall my help come? My help comes from the Lord who made heaven and earth."* According to this Psalm the believer who needs help during a time of great challenge has put his or her trust in the Lord God. And, in verses 3-8, the believer is assured that God can be trusted to meet him or her in their time of great need.

This is a great Psalm for us believers who are consumed with pain and hurt. Because the Psalmist reminds us to take our focus off the loss of our precious loved one and place our focus on the one who made the heavens and the earth, who is our Great and Mighty God. As believers, we our reminded to worship our glorious God in our time of great need. He will not let you slip; He will keep you man and woman of God.

In this time of your great loss put your total trust in Him and not on your pain and hurt. Worship by lifting your eyes totally on the mountains (i.e., on God's creation) from which your help comes because the help that you need during this time of precious loss comes from Him who made the heaven and the earth. Turn your pain to gain through your worship of Him!

Reflection on God:

_____
_____
_____
_____
_____
_____
_____
_____
_____
_____
_____
_____
_____
_____
_____
_____
_____
_____
_____
_____
_____
_____
_____
_____
_____
_____
_____
_____
_____
_____
_____
_____
_____
_____

Psalm 100

1 Shout joyfully to the Lord, all the earth. 2 Serve the Lord with gladness; Come before Him with joyful singing. 3 Know that the Lord Himself is God; It is He who has made us, and not we ourselves; We are His people and the sheep of His pasture.
4 Enter His gates with thanksgiving, And His courts with praise. Give thanks to Him, bless His name. 5 For the Lord is good; His lovingkindness is everlasting, And His faithfulness to all generations.

DAY 32 The God to Praise

This Psalm is a call to praise and worship. The psalmist opens with, *"Shout joyfully to the Lord, all the earth. Serve the Lord with gladness; Come before Him with joyful singing."* (vs. 1-2) When you come to this Psalm, notice the seven descriptions of praise and worship: *shout joyfully, gladness, singing, thanksgiving, praise, be thankful, and bless.* This is great news for all believers because with these seven descriptions of praise and worship, this is a Psalm that will bring you tremendous comfort in the time of great hurt as you praise and worship Him.

This is not only a Psalm that calls one to praise and worship. It is also a Psalm that gives the reason for so doing. Why? *"Know that the Lord Himself is God; It is He who has made us, and not we ourselves."* (vs. 3) When you as a believer loses a precious loved one and your heart and soul is hurting deeply, you are called by your God to praise and worship Him. Why? Because He knows all about you and what you are experiencing during this most critical time in your life. He is the only one who can and will turn your pain into gain for His Glory through the precious means that He has given you – PRAISE AND WORSHIP. Use it man and woman of God. You are precious in His sight, and He wants you to turn to Him. Trust Him man and woman of God. He is God and He made you!

History records when Melancthon was mourning the death of his beloved son in Dresden, July 1559, not long before his own death, he drew comfort from the 3rd verse, *"It is he that hath made us, and not we ourselves: we are His people, and the sheep of His pasture."*

My fellow child of God, respond to the call of our God to praise and worship!

Reflection on God:

_____
_____
_____
_____
_____
_____
_____
_____
_____
_____
_____
_____
_____
_____
_____
_____
_____
_____
_____
_____
_____
_____
_____
_____
_____
_____
_____
_____
_____
_____
_____
_____

Psalm 63

1 O God, You are my God; I shall seek You earnestly; My soul thirsts for You, my flesh yearns for You, In a dry and weary land where there is no water. 2 Thus I have seen You in the sanctuary, to see Your Power and Your glory. 3 Because Your lovingkindness is better than life, my lips will praise You. 4 So I will bless You as long as I live; I will lift up my hands in Your name. 5 My soul is satisfied as with marrow and fatness, and my mouth offers praises with joyful lips.

6 When I remember you on my bed, I meditate on You in the night watches, 7 For You have been my help, and in the shadow of Your wings I sing for joy.

8 My soul clings to You; Your right hand upholds me.

9 But those who seek my life to destroy it, Will go into the depths of the earth. 10 They will be delivered over to the power of the sword; They will be a prey for foxes. 11 But the king will rejoice in God; Everyone who swears by Him will glory, For the mouths of those who speak lies will be stopped.

DAY 33 Worshipping God when it Appears you Cannot

This is a beautiful Psalm because it records and describes the heart of King David when he was driven out into the wilderness, and he had no access to the sanctuary where he could worship the Lord God. However, during this difficult and lonely time, he fed upon the remembrance of God Almighty amid his time of challenge. David's heart is described in verse 1-2:

"O God, You are my God; I shall seek You earnestly; My soul thirsts for You, my flesh yearns for You, In a dry and weary land where there is no water. Thus, I have seen You in the sanctuary, To see Your Power and Your glory."

In a time of David's struggle and hurt as he dealt with his own son wanting to kill him, he chose to reflect on his remembrance of the glory his God who is the only one who could bring him comfort and peace. David declares in verses 3-6:

*"Because Your lovingkindness is better than life, my lips will praise You. So, I will bless You as long as I live;
I will lift up my hands in Your name.
My soul is satisfied as with marrow and fatness, and my mouth offers praises with joyful lips.
When I remember you on my bed,
I meditate on You in the night watches."*

People of God, when it appears that you cannot worship your God because the pain is so severe, take the action of your beloved brother David and reflect on all the days you worshipped Him in the past and how great and marvelous He has been and is to you today. David stated in verses 7-8, *"For You have been my help, and in the shadow of Your wings I sing for joy. My soul clings to You; Your right hand upholds me."* David's remembrance of what God had done for him in the past enables him to form his resolve for the future.

My beloved child of God, during this time of great hurt and loss follow the will and mind of David who allowed our God to turn his pain into gain through worship. You are hurting deeply. But, let God bring you out of this great hurt by reflecting and worshipping Him for His marvelous help!

Hallelujah

Reflection on God:

_____
_____
_____
_____
_____
_____
_____
_____
_____
_____
_____
_____
_____
_____
_____
_____
_____
_____
_____
_____
_____
_____
_____
_____
_____
_____
_____
_____
_____
_____

Psalm 71:5-9, 14

5 For You are my hope Oh Lord God, You are my confidence from my youth. 6 By You I have been sustained from my birth; You are He who took me from my mother's womb; My praise is continually of You. 7 I have become a marvel to many, For You are my strong refuge. 8 My mouth is filled with Your praise And with Your glory all day long. 9 Do not cast me off in the time of old age; Do not forsake me when my strength fails.

14 But I will hope continually and will yet praise Thee more and more.

Day 34 My Hope when it is Dark

This is such a unique Psalm because it depicts the strength and character of an old-aged saint of God who has a tremendous and wonderful history with our glorious and great God. In a time of great trouble, he believes that God has been his hope and trust from the time that he was born through to his old age. *"O Lord God, You are my confidence from my youth. By You I have been sustained from my birth; You are He who took me from my mother's womb; My praise is continually of You"* (vs. 5-6).

Old age had taken its toll on his life, attacking his faith and walk with God over the many years. However, his strength in the Lord persevered through his praise and worship of God Almighty. He declares this wonderful reality in verses 7-8: *"I have become a marvel to many, For You are my strong refuge. My mouth is filled with Your praise And with Your glory all day long."* In verse 14, he further proclaims this incredible truth: *"But I will continually and will yet praise Thee more and more."* For the believer, despair, and despondence in the time of hurt and challenge does not have to become a reality, though it often does. Our God desires you to be a great witness of his glory and sustaining power through the precious means of praise and worship.

The psalmist promises to be a witness of God's faithfulness by worshipping Him with his mouth more and more. Man and woman of God, be led by the powerful Holy Spirit that dwells in you to praise and worship your God during this time of great hurt and pain. *"Greater is He that is in you than he that is in the world"* (1 John 4:4).

Reflection on God:

_____
_____
_____
_____
_____
_____
_____
_____
_____
_____
_____
_____
_____
_____
_____
_____
_____
_____
_____
_____
_____
_____
_____
_____
_____
_____
_____
_____
_____
_____
_____

Psalm 95:1-7

1 O come, let us sing for joy to the Lord, let us shout joyfully to the rock of our salvation. 2 Let us come before His presence with thanksgiving, let us shout joyfully to Him with psalms. 3 For the Lord is a great God And a great King above all gods, 4 In whose hand are the depths of the earth, The peaks of the mountains are His also. 5 The sea is His, for it was He who made it, And His hands formed the dry land.
6 Come, let us worship and bow down, let us kneel before the Lord our Maker. 7 For He is our God, and we are the people of His pasture and the sheep of His hand.

DAY 35 When God Calls, He Enables

The dominating fact of this Psalm is that "The LORD Reigns," and this fact calls for a celebration from the people of God. No matter what circumstance the saint of God finds himself or herself in, the Psalmist opens this great Psalm with a compelling invitation: *"O come, let us sing for joy to the Lord, let us shout joyfully to the rock of our salvation. Let us come before His presence with thanksgiving, let us shout joyfully to Him with psalms."*

The call is to exultation — a call to worship. It is a call of exultation that led to adoration. The transformation from exultation to adoration is made very naturally for the believer. Because when a believer reflects on the awesomeness of God, it compels him or her to respond in worship of exultation and adoration.

Listen to what the Psalmist says in verses 3-6: *"For the Lord is a great God and a great King above all gods, in whose hand are the depths of the earth, the peaks of the mountains are His also. The sea is His, for it was He who made it, and His hands formed the dry land. Come, let us worship and bow down, let us kneel before the Lord our Maker."*

There are experiences in life that can cause a believer to take his or her focus off the psalmist's description in verses 3-5. The loss of a precious loved one is perhaps the number one devastating experience that causes such a misplacement of a believer's focus.

This Psalm is a call to the believer who is experiencing the excessive pain of loss to turn his or her focus back onto the awesomeness of God. This call to worship is for you to tap into your God-given ability to respond with praise and worship. This response to worship is driven by the words of the Psalmist in verse 7: *"For He is our God, and we are the people of His pasture and the sheep of His hand."*

God has created believers in the time of sorrow to worship Him. Job taught this fact with assurance: *"The Lord gave, and the Lord has taken away. Blessed be the name of the Lord."* (Job 1:21)

During this time of your precious loss do not allow yourself to become consumed by your loss and, in doing so, lose your focus on your great creator, God. He is the God of all comfort. Worship and adore Him! When you adore Him, it will turn the pain of your loss into gain.

To God be the Glory!

Reflection on God:

_____
_____
_____
_____
_____
_____
_____
_____
_____
_____
_____
_____
_____
_____
_____
_____
_____
_____
_____
_____
_____
_____
_____
_____
_____
_____
_____
_____
_____
_____
_____
_____
_____

Psalm 105:1-5

1 Oh give thanks to the Lord, call upon His name;
Make known His deeds among the peoples.
2 Sing to Him, sing praises to Him;
Speak of all His wonders.
3 Glory in His holy name;
Let the heart of those who seek the Lord be glad.
4 Seek the Lord and His strength;
Seek His face continually.
5 Remember His wonders which He has done,
His marvels and the judgments uttered by His mouth.

DAY 36 Glory ye in His Holy Name

This Psalm is a Hallelujah Psalm. It begins with a Hallelujah: *"O give thanks unto the LORD"* (vs. 1), and it ends with a Hallelujah: *"Praise ye the LORD"* (vs. 45).

This Psalm highlights the greatness and glory of God almighty. His marvelous works and unmatched attributes summon believers to extol who He is. Because of this, the Psalmist calls upon believers to praise and to proclaim His greatness through worship. We are to sing, to talk, to glorify, to rejoice, to seek, and to remember how marvelous He is and how powerful He has been in our life.

As I stated, this is a Hallelujah Psalm. What does that mean to the believer? "Hallelujah" is a word reserved for the people of God who were delivered by God from their enemies. It is used in the Old Testament (Psalms 104-109 & 113-118) and in the New Testament (Revelation 19:1, 3, 4, & 6) for the people to praise Him for delivering them from their oppressors. "Hallelujah" is proclaimed after the judgment of the ungodly; and "Hallelujah" is proclaimed as praise by the people of God for deliverance. So, when you say Hallelujah, it has rich and special meaning.

God has made a covenant with His people whom He has called. His word, His oath, and His law have declared that He is everlasting throughout all generations. He promised to never leave you nor forsake you in any form or fashion (Hebrews 13:5). He will be there for you and with you through your darkest and most trying experiences in life. So, when the excruciating pain of loss takes over your heart, mind, body, and soul, you have only one recourse, which is your God-given response: Give God a Hallelujah praise! Praise Him for deliverance from this pain that seeks to overtake you. You have the power to release yourself and be delivered from this indescribable pain and deep hurt through worship by shouting HALLELUJAH to God Almighty!

God desires to deliver you from your pain and hurt, and He will keep His promise to do so through the object of your obedience to His statutes right in the midst of it. Man or woman of God, I implore you to tap into your God-given help – His Holy Spirit, and let it out.

Begin and end this experience in the exact way that Psalm 105 begins and ends – with a Hallelujah praise!

Shout

because

God's so good

Reflection on God:

_____

_____

_____

_____

_____

_____

_____

_____

_____

_____

_____

_____

_____

_____

_____

_____

_____

_____

_____

_____

_____

_____

_____

_____

_____

_____

_____

_____

_____

_____

_____

_____

_____

Psalm 145:1-3

1 I will extol You, my God, O King, And I will bless Your name forever and ever. 2 Every day I will bless You, And I will praise Your name forever and ever. 3 Great is the LORD, and highly to be praised, And His greatness is unsearchable.

DAY 37 God is Great, Good, Glorious and Gracious

This is a Psalm where human resolve and Divine purpose interlock. This is a Psalm of praise. *"I will"* occurs six times in the entire Psalm (vss. 1-21); *"praise"* occurs four times; *"bless"* occurs four times; and *"LORD"* occurs nine times. Believers are to extol, bless, and praise the LORD our God (vss. 1-3). The Psalmist, who says "I will" multiple times, resolved in his heart to praise and worship Him every day and forever and ever, regularly and perpetually; and he will do it fervently for the LORD is greatly to be praised. God is great every day no matter what the circumstance or hurt a believer may be experiencing. Praising His greatness and goodness is the key to overcoming the circumstance and hurt.

"Cry aloud and shout for joy, O inhabitant of Zion, for great in your midst is the Holy One of Israel." (Isaiah 12:6). The prophet Isaiah is instructing the saint of God to praise and worship Him in your most difficult of circumstances. Why? *"For great in your midst is the Holy One of Israel."* Those who belong to Him, find Him to be good at all times. Although many will not praise Him, those who belong to Him will bless and worship His Holy name, and, no matter what, they will *"cry aloud and shout for joy."*

The Psalmist in this beautiful and sweet Psalm 145 is calling you to worship Him and let your heart be filled with the presence of your great God in the midst of your tremendous pain and be led to worship with the resolve of the Psalmist: *"I will extol you, my God O King, and I will bless Your name forever and ever, every day is will bless You, and I praise Your name forever and ever. Great is the LORD, and highly to be praised and His greatness is unsearchable."*

In verses 18-20, the Psalmist mentions three conditions of blessing His name: 1) call upon Him, 2) fear Him, and 3) love Him. In your time of loss and severe hurt, it is important to remember these three conditions. God is nigh. He is right there with you and within you. Worship Him and call on His name because you fear (reverence) Him and, most of all, because you love Him and you know that He loves you. He is on record declaring that He will turn your pain into gain. *"You will keep him in perfect peace whose mind is stayed on you."* (Isaiah 26:3 NKJV)

The Psalmist concludes this glorious, great, and gracious Psalm with words of his resolve that is to be the resolve and testimony of all believers:

> *"My mouth will speak the praise of the LORD,*
> *And all flesh will bless His Holy name forever*
> *and ever."* (vs. 21)

Reflection on God:

_____
_____
_____
_____
_____
_____
_____
_____
_____
_____
_____
_____
_____
_____
_____
_____
_____
_____
_____
_____
_____
_____
_____
_____
_____
_____
_____
_____
_____
_____
_____
_____
_____

Psalm 68:32-35

32 Sing to God, O kingdoms of the earth,
Sing praises to the Lord.
33 To Him who rides upon the highest heavens, which are
from ancient times;
Behold, He speaks forth with His voice, a mighty voice.
34 Ascribe strength to God;
His majesty is over Israel and His strength is in the skies.
35 O God, You are awesome from Your sanctuary.
The God of Israel Himself gives strength and power to the
people. Blessed be God!

Day 38 Draw Strength from the God of your Salvation

During a believer's deepest time of hurt, he or she must be reminded of the greatness and awesomeness of God. In Psalm 68, the Psalmist does this in a superb way. He compels believers to rush to a triumphant praise of God's unsurpassed and unequalled love for His own. In this Psalm, you are brought face to face with the glorious awesomeness of God.

I love this stanza of the Psalm. It begins with *"Sing unto God"* and it ends with *"Blessed be God."* The Psalmist's worship of God is dependent upon His awesomeness as he states, *"You are awesome."* (vs. 35) The Lord is victor in all things and those who belong to Him are the crowned and the benefactors of His triumph through praising and worshipping His awesomeness. The great truth of this Psalm is that God is the strength of His own, those of us who are believers. The word "strength" is mentioned three times in the last two verses of this incredible Psalm.

Dear man or woman of God, during this time of grief, remember that your awesome God is your strength in the time of great need. The Prophet Isaiah reminds of this marvelous fact when he writes, *"He gives strength to the weary, and to him who lacks might He increases power."* (Isaiah 40:29). It is your good pleasure to trust Him and bless His name through worship, ascribing to your strength in Him. Your victory during this difficult time is in the victory and sovereignty of God. He is an awesome God; He is a God of strength; and He is God who gives this strength to the believer who will draw on this strength through worship. Let Him do what He does best – carry you through this time of hurt and turn your pain into gain for His Glory and your blessing. *"Blessed be God!"*

Reflection on God:

_____
_____
_____
_____
_____
_____
_____
_____
_____
_____
_____
_____
_____
_____
_____
_____
_____
_____
_____
_____
_____
_____
_____
_____
_____
_____
_____
_____
_____
_____
_____
_____
_____
_____

Psalm 34:17-19

17 The righteous cry, and the Lord hears and delivers them out of all their troubles. 18 The Lord is near to the brokenhearted and saves those who are crushed in spirit. 19 Many are the afflictions of the righteous, but the Lord delivers him out of them all.

Day 39 Rejoice! You are Delivered from your Pain

The title of this Psalm is "Thanksgiving for Deliverance." This Psalm and its title are not to be separated. This is a Psalm of praise for complete deliverance. The Psalmist, King David, is extremely grateful for his mighty deliverance by God from his devastating hurt. This is the reason for the incredible words in verse 1: "*I will bless the LORD at all times; His praise shall continually be in my mouth.*" David bears the richness of his experience through God's mercy and continual love for him. This Psalm reminds believers of what we must do to be blessed by the almighty God:

1) In the time of need, seek Him through worship and be delivered. "*I sought the LORD, and He answered me, and delivered me from all my fears.*" (vs.4)

2) Look to God and be enlightened. "*They looked to Him and were radiant.*" (vs. 5)

3) Cry out and be brought out of your troubles. "*This poor man cried, and the LORD heard him, and saved him out of all his troubles.*" (vs. 6)

4) Fear Him and He will surround you and recue you. "*The angel of the LORD encamps around those who fear Him, and recues them.*" (vs. 7)

Therefore, your deliverance in the time of hurt is conditioned on your worship and praise. God cannot do what He would unless you do what you should. He is drawing you to Him. He is calling you to get down to the business of worshipping Him. Christianity is not a dream, but a life; it is not a conception, but a character. You can only be victorious and delivered as you get out of self and tap into the greatness of what God has put inside of you, His Holy Spirit. During this time of great pain and loss, "*Do not quench the Spirit.*" In other words, do not ignore Him. (1 Thessalonians 5:19)

Please focus on what God says He will do for you in verses 17-19: "*The righteous cry, and the LORD hears and delivers that out of all their troubles. The LORD is near to the brokenhearted and saves those who are crushed in spirit. Many are the afflictions of the righteous, but the LORD delivers him out of them all."*

The wonderful and amazing reality of Psalm 34: 17-19 is that God declares to you that He knows your heart is broken and crushed as a result of your loss, and He beckons you to trust Him and allow Him to turn your pain into gain. Do not let your heart be troubled, but trust the work of the Divine mercy and power of God to deliver you.

To God be the Glory!

THE
RIGHTEOUS
sings
&
rejoices

· PROVERBS 29:6 ·

Reflection on God:

_____
_____
_____
_____
_____
_____
_____
_____
_____
_____
_____
_____
_____
_____
_____
_____
_____
_____
_____
_____
_____
_____
_____
_____
_____
_____
_____
_____
_____
_____
_____
_____
_____
_____
_____
_____

Isaiah 12:2-6

2 "Behold, God is my salvation, I will trust and not be afraid; For the Lord God is my strength and song, And He has become my salvation." 3 Therefore you will joyously draw water from the springs of salvation. 4 And in that day you will say, "Give thanks to the Lord, call on His name. Make known His deeds among the peoples; Make them remember that His name is exalted." 5 Praise the Lord in song, for He has done excellent things; Let this be known throughout the earth. 6 Cry aloud and shout for joy, O inhabitant of Zion, for great in your midst is the Holy One of Israel.

DAY 40 Expressing my Praise to God

In Isaiah 12, the prophet is declaring that the remnant of God will bless the Lord for His greatness, goodness, salvation and comfort. And will call on each other to remember who He is, what He has done, and that He is to be exalted. He is a God that will fulfill His promises to His own. And the people of God will respond in praise because of His glorious deeds. *"Praise the LORD in song, for He has done excellent things; Let this be known throughout the earth. Cry aloud and shout for joy, O inhabitant of Zion, for great in your midst is the Holy One of Israel."*

It is very important for the believer to always know and be confident that God is with you during your most difficult periods in life. *"For great in your midst is the Holy One of Israel."* You are not alone in this pain that you are experiencing right at this moment in your life. As the Prophet testifies, God is right there in the middle of it all, and He wants to bless you through it. In this time of great challenge, as a believer, do not be afraid but rest completely in God and place full reliance upon His promise to help you, and do not be afraid. *"Therefore, you will joyously draw water from the springs of salvation. And in that day you will say, Give thanks to the LORD, call on His name."* (vs. 3-4)

The most compelling aspect of this scripture and what a believer must focus on during the time of pain and hurt is that God is with you, and He has not and will not forsake you. *"Great in your midst is the Holy One of Israel."* He is there as the Giver of victory in your deepest time of need. *"Cry out and shout,"* to Him. Let Him show you His miraculous power during this time of great need in your life.

My love, Alicia, and I pray with all sincerity that you will let God do for you what He did for us and for all the saints of God throughout history by turning the pain of loss into a gain. Be blessed in the Lord!

Reflection on God:

_____
_____
_____
_____
_____
_____
_____
_____
_____
_____
_____
_____
_____
_____
_____
_____
_____
_____
_____
_____
_____
_____
_____
_____
_____
_____
_____
_____
_____
_____
_____
_____
_____
_____
_____
_____
_____
_____

Made in the USA
Middletown, DE
11 March 2022

62468188R00080